Sophia Finds a Geocache

ISBN: **1540450341**
ISBN-13: **978-1540450340**

DEDICATED TO SOPHIA

May all your adventures be epic!

Tribute to North Dakota, USA Geocachers

A special thank you goes out to all ND geocachers, those in our home state who have placed the majority of the caches we have found, allowing us to enjoy the history, views, and beauty of the Great Plains. Plus, both of us, the author and illustrator, grew up here in ND. As a tribute to you, we have included seven North Dakota state symbols hidden in this book (a scavenger hunt inside the story of a treasure hunt): Northern Pike (State Fish), Milk (State Beverage), Western Meadowlark (State Bird), Chokecherry (State Fruit), American Elm (State Tree), Prairie Rose (State Flower), and Ladybug (State Bug). Good luck!

Summer break was almost over, and Sophia still needed to have an adventure. Finley adopted a puppy. Everly went to dance camp. Nolan traveled to Fun Land. Sophia wanted to do something really awesome before school started.

"Sophia, what are you doing inside? Go have fun with your friends." Sophia's mom said as she poked her head into Sophia's room.

"Everyone is doing cool things this summer. I've only taken care of the neighbor's cat," Sophia said.

"But you earned $20!"

Sophia shrugged.

"Well, how about you and I go geocaching?" Sophia's mom said.

"What's geocaching?" asked Sophia.

"It's a real world treasure hunt. Grab a few small toys you don't play with anymore and meet me downstairs."

Sophia and her mom sat at the computer and went to geocaching.com to create a secret geocaching user name. They watched a short movie, during which Sophia started jumping up and down with excitement.

They downloaded the app on Sophia's mom's phone, logged in with their secret name, and saw that a nearby park had a good beginner geocache in it. Sophia hit "start" to get directions to the geocache. They hopped in their car and followed the map.

"When we get to the park, we have to be extra careful to not attract muggles' attention," said Sophia's mom.

"What are muggles and why should we hide from them?" asked Sophia.

"Muggles are people who don't know what geocaching is. To make the game more fun and keep it among members, we want to stay like spies," replied Sophia's mom.

"Cool, I'm going to pretend I'm an undercover gopher photographer! Mom, here's our turn!"

Sophia's mom parked the car. Spring Lake Park was busy. Muggle grownups were frolfing. Muggle kids were swimming in the lake and climbing on the playground equipment. Muggle dogs were playing fetch in the Bark Zone.

Sophia and her mom grabbed the cell phone and backpack with a pencil, small toys, and water bottles in it. They made their way to the trailhead.

"Ok, Sophia, since we downloaded the app at home and decided on a geocache to find, let's look at the geocache's page and check out the details again."

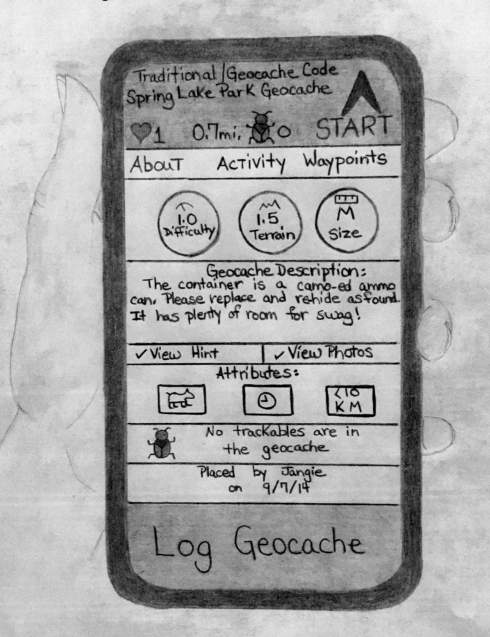

"After re-reading the description, we know we're looking for a shoebox-sized container that is camouflaged in some way. Let's follow the trail. You can hold the phone and navigate using the compass," said Sophia's mom.

"Wow! Some muggles were messy hikers. They didn't throw away their snacks' wrappers. Good thing I brought this bag! While walking the trail, we can collect trash," said Sophia's mom. "This is called CITO, Cache In Trash Out, and it helps keep our game board, the earth, clean."

"Mom, we're 20 feet away from the geocache!" Sophia shouted.

"Great! Now let's put down the phone and look around for anything out of place," said Sophia's mom.

"I found it! It was right under this pile of sticks!" Sophia yelled. She opened up the box and discovered all kinds of treasure!

Sophia's Toys   Geocache's Swag

"Way to go! If you want, trade one of your toys for a swag item,"
said Sophia's mom, "but make sure to trade fairly. I'll sign our secret
name in the log book."

"Since you're done trading toys, we'll hide the geocache again so other geocachers can have fun finding it too. Plus, we don't want muggles accidently finding it and possibly moving it," explained Sophia's mom.

"Mom, muggles!" Sophia said while pointing at a boy walking his dog.

"Shhh...let's pretend we're taking a selfie," Sophia's mom said.

Once the boy and his dog were further down the trail, Sophia and her mom started walking back to their car.

"That was so much fun, Mom! We cleaned up the park, found a box of toys, and hid from a muggle. Best day of summer vacation!"

Sophia and her mom got into their car and buckled up.

"I can't wait to tell all my friends about our adventure," said Sophia, "and show them my new necklace!"

"I hope we can go geocaching tomorrow!"

A Beginner's Guide to Geocaching

<u>Definition:</u> Geocaching is the recreational activity of hunting for and finding a hidden object by means of GPS coordinates posted on a website.

Geocaching.com has all the information you need to get started, and social media can help you in the form of blogs, YouTube videos, podcasts, Periscopes, Twitter, Instagram, Facebook, and more.

Geocaches can be any size, from a fake screw to a large shed. Multiple types exist too. The geocache in this book is a traditional geocache, but some involve solving puzzles, answering questions about the earth, or attending an event, so make sure you know what type you're targeting before you start the search. The difficulty and terrain are important factors to read about as well. Geocaches can be found all over the world, under water, suspended in air, inside caves, on top of mountains, and possibly in a parking lot near you.

Trackables are also a neat feature of geocaching. Sophia didn't find one of these in the book, but you can discover a trackable code within the story's pages! Trackables involve using a code online to track an item (or person) around the world. The most popular form of a trackable is a metal dog tag with a travel bug icon and a hitchhiker, a small toy, attached with a keychain. Please make sure you know how to discover, grab, and drop these game pieces during your adventures.

Lastly, please be respectful of geocaches, geocachers, and the places geocaching takes you. Geocaching is a free game to play, which means people are not paid to place and maintain their containers.

We wish you epic adventures and lots of treasure in your future!

About the Author

Angie Westphal and her husband, Jon (aka Jangie), grew up in a small western town in North Dakota, where they now raise their daughter, Sophia. They are often seen at sporting events and enjoying nature. Angie graduated from the University of North Dakota with a Bachelor of Arts in English. Follow Angie's geocaching adventures on Twitter, Facebook, and Instagram with @GeoJangie or on her blog: www.GeocachingJangie.com.

About the Illustrator

Michele Goebel has lived most of her life in North Dakota with her husband, Ken Goebel. They like going on walks in the great outdoors and spending time with their four children, Angie, Thomas, Elizabeth, and John, as well as their granddaughter, Sophia. Michele has always loved art, whether taking classes or coloring with crayons with her kids. She's happy to create and share it again.

Made in the USA
Monee, IL
06 December 2020